CELEBRATING HOLIDAYS

Chinese New Year

by Rachel Grack

BELLWETHER MEDIA • MINNEAPOLIS, MN

Note to Librarians, Teachers, and Parents:

Blastoff! Readers are carefully developed by literacy experts and combine standards-based content with developmentally appropriate text.

Level 1 provides the most support through repetition of high-frequency words, light text, predictable sentence patterns, and strong visual support.

Level 2 offers early readers a bit more challenge through varied simple sentences, increased text load, and less repetition of high-frequency words.

Level 3 advances early-fluent readers toward fluency through increased text and concept load, less reliance on visuals, longer sentences, and more literary language.

Level 4 builds reading stamina by providing more text per page, increased use of punctuation, greater variation in sentence patterns, and increasingly challenging vocabulary.

Level 5 encourages children to move from "learning to read" to "reading to learn" by providing even more text, varied writing styles, and less familiar topics.

Whichever book is right for your reader, Blastoff! Readers are the perfect books to build confidence and encourage a love of reading that will last a lifetime!

This edition first published in 2017 by Bellwether Media, Inc.

Library of Congress Cataloging-in-Publication Data

Names: Koestler-Grack, Rachel A., 1973- author.
Title: Chinese New Year / by Rachel Grack.
Description: Minneapolis, MN : Bellwether Media, Inc., 2017. | Series: Blastoff! Readers: Celebrating Holidays | Includes bibliographical references and index. | Audience: Ages: 5-8. | Audience: Grades: K to Grade 3.
Identifiers: LCCN 2016033344 (print) | LCCN 2016035230 (ebook) | ISBN 9781626175914 (hardcover : alk. paper) | ISBN 9781681033211 (ebook)
Subjects: LCSH: Chinese New Year–Juvenile literature. | Chinese New Year–History–Juvenile literature.
Classification: LCC GT4905 .K64 2017 (print) | LCC GT4905 (ebook) | DDC 394.261–dc23
LC record available at https://lccn.loc.gov/2016033344

Editor: Christina Leaf   Designer: Lois Stanfield

Printed in the United States of America, North Mankato, MN.

Table of Contents

Happy Chinese New Year!

Beautiful **lanterns** light up streets under the full moon.

lanterns

4

lion dancers

Firecrackers pop while lions
and dragons dance in a parade.
Happy Chinese New Year!

What Is Chinese New Year?

Chinese New Year, or Spring **Festival**, celebrates spring's arrival. People focus on family and good luck. To prepare, they clean, shop, and decorate.

Animal Years

Each Chinese year is linked with a different animal. The animals repeat every 12 years.

2017	鸡	Rooster
2018	狗	Dog
2019	猪	Pig
2020	鼠	Rat
2021	牛	Ox
2022	虎	Tiger
2023	兔	Rabbit
2024	龙	Dragon
2025	蛇	Snake
2026	马	Horse
2027	羊	Goat
2028	猴	Monkey

Chinese New Year is China's biggest holiday.

China

N
W E
S

Chinese New Year in London, U.K.

Much of Asia celebrates it as **Lunar** New Year. Cities around the world may also throw big celebrations.

Chinese New Year Beginnings

Chinese stories tell of a monster, Nian, that attacked villages.

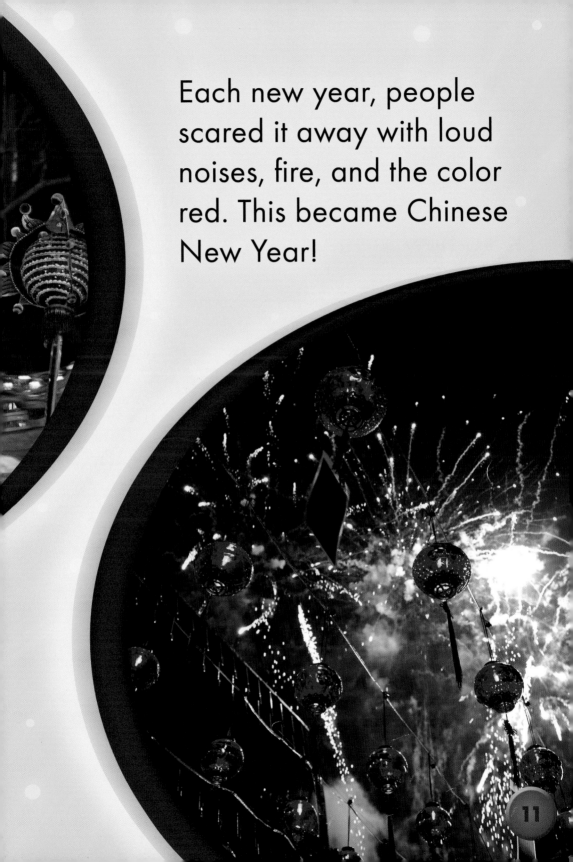

Each new year, people scared it away with loud noises, fire, and the color red. This became Chinese New Year!

11

Time to Celebrate

Chinese New Year begins on a new moon.

full moon

How Do You Say?

English Phrase	Characters	Pronunciation
Happy Chinese New Year	过年好	go KNEE-an how
Happy Spring Festival	春节快乐	ChUN jee-ay KWAI leh
Good luck	福	foo
Wishing good luck	恭喜发财	GOHNG-she FAH-cai

It always falls between January 21 and February 20. It ends on the full moon.

Chinese New Year Traditions!

To celebrate, people decorate doors with spring **couplets**.

← couplets →

14

The short sayings share
wisdom. The red **banners**
bring good luck and joy.

Adults give children red
envelopes for luck. They tuck
new money inside. Many
write happy notes, too.

Make a Red Envelope

You can make red envelopes for your family and friends. Write them messages to wish joy or luck!

What You Need:
- red construction paper
- scissors
- ruler
- glue stick
- 3-inch by 5-inch index cards
- colored markers
- gold glitter glue

What You Do:

1. With the red paper, cut out a shape like the one pictured below.

2. Fold the two short flaps in toward the center of the paper.

3. Fold the big flap up to meet the other two and glue the big flap to the shorter flaps.

4. Write a message on an index card with colored markers.

5. Slide the card into the envelope.

6. Fold the top flap to close the envelope and glue.

7. Decorate the front with glitter glue. Try writing the Chinese character Fu (福) for good luck!

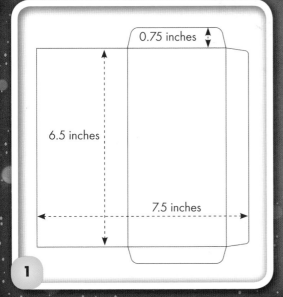

0.75 inches

6.5 inches

7.5 inches

1

3

7

Celebrating families eat special foods for luck, health, and **wealth**.

dumplings

They serve fish, long noodles, and oranges. **Dumplings** and rice cakes are also popular.

Chinese New Year ends with the Lantern Festival. Lights, puppets, and dancers parade through streets. Animal-shaped lanterns shine brightly.

People are ready for a lucky
new year!

Glossary

banners—strips of cloth or paper with words or pictures on them

couplets—Chinese poetry made up of two short lines that often wish good luck

dumplings—Chinese food made of dough wrappers stuffed with meat or vegetables; dumplings are steamed, fried, or boiled.

festival—a celebration

lanterns—covered lights that can be hung or carried

lunar—related to the moon

wealth—riches or money

To Learn More

AT THE LIBRARY
Otto, Carolyn. *Celebrate Chinese New Year.*
Washington, D.C.: National Geographic, 2009.

Tang, Sanmu. *Celebrating the Chinese New Year.*
Shanghai, China: Shanghai Press, 2010.

Tang, Sanmu. *Celebrating the Lantern Festival.*
Shanghai, China: Shanghai Press, 2010.

ON THE WEB
Learning more about
Chinese New Year is
as easy as 1, 2, 3.

1. Go to www.factsurfer.com.

2. Enter "Chinese New Year" into the search box.

3. Click the "Surf" button and you will see a
   list of related web sites.

With factsurfer.com, finding more
information is just a click away.

Index

The images in this book are reproduced through the courtesy of: Babyboom, front cover; CHANKC, p. 4; coward_lion, pp. 4-5; nvelichko, pp. 6-7; animicsgo, p. 7 (icons); AwaylGl, p. 8; RealyEasyStar/ Rodolfo Felici/ Alamy, p. 9; Judy Bellah/ Alamy, pp. 10-11; beltsazar, p. 11; zyxeos30, p. 12; Yao Sheng Bo, p. 14; View Stock/ Alamy, pp. 14-15, 16; Lois Stanfield, p. 17 (all); SKY2015, p. 18 (left); Suppakrit Boonsat, pp. 18 (right), 20; CB2/ ZOB/ WENN/ Newscom, pp. 18-19; Sergei Bachlakov, p. 21.